SCHIRMER'S LIBRARY
OF MUSICAL CLASSICS

Vol. 1975

Ludwig van Beethoven

Notturno

For Viola and Piano

Revised and edited by Sydney Beck

ISBN 978-0-7935-2022-0

G. SCHIRMER, Inc.

DISTRIBUTED BY

HAL•LEONARD®
CORPORATION
7777 W. BLUEMOUND RD. P.O. BOX 13819 MILWAUKEE, WI 53213

NOTE

Late in 1803, apparently at the solicitation of Franz Anton Hoffmeister, the Leipzig publisher, Beethoven agreed to sell to the firm of Hoffmeister & Kühnel nearly a dozen compositions, most of which were minor or insignificant works. He was obviously in need of money.[1] That Hoffmeister gladly took almost anything from the master at this time in the hope of acquiring from him a few choicer items for his catalogue, is evident from the low quality of some of the music he was willing to accept. Although this particular lot included the manuscripts of the Romance in G for Violin and Orchestra, the parts for the Prometheus Overture, and the XIV Variations for Piano, Violin, and Violoncello (which became Op. 40, 43, and 44 respectively), the bulk of the material was hardly worthy of the great composer. Furthermore, at least three of the works had already been published, and two were arrangements of earlier compositions.

Of the arrangements, in which we are interested here, the first to appear was the Serenade for Flute (or Violin) and Piano, Op. 41,[2] originally the Serenade for Flute, Violin, and Viola, Op. 25; the second, published a short time later,[3] was the Notturno for Pianoforte and Viola, Op. 42, after the String Trio, Op. 8.

Who actually made these arrangements has never been established. Some writers have attributed them to the composer himself despite the fact that the title pages of both editions read "Arrangé . . . et *revûe* par l'Auteur".[4] It is interesting to note that the first thematic catalogue of Beethoven's works, published during his lifetime,[5] lists them as "Arrangée . . . par l'Auteur", and that in a similar catalogue issued by Breitkopf & Härtel (Leipzig, 1851) they are still referred to as arrangements "vom Componisten"; while, in a revision of the latter catalogue made by G. Nottebohm (1868),[6] this assertion is flatly contradicted with the statement that the composer merely looked them over and made a few changes.[7] Nottebohm based his opinion on the letter to Hoffmeister of September 22, 1803[8], in which, presumably[9] referring to the arrangements of his trios, Beethoven wrote: "The transcriptions[9] are not my own but I have looked through them and in places improved them. Therefore, I am not willing to have you state that I made them, for that would be a lie and besides, I could find neither the time nor the patience for such work."[10] This view was apparently later taken up by A. W. Thayer, the celebrated biographer of the composer, in the second volume of his work (1872), for, in his catalogue of 1865,[11] he was still uncertain about the authorship of the arrangements, at least as far as Op. 41 was

[1] With reference to this transaction, Beethoven wrote to Hoffmeister, in a letter dated Vienna, September 22, 1803: "The best thing I can wish you is prosperity, and I would willingly give you everything as a gift, if by so doing I could get along. But, only reflect that everyone here around me has a post and knows that he has enough to live on, but good Heavens, where would one place a *parvum talentum cum ego* at the Imperial Court?"

[2] The new opus numbers were assigned by the publisher.

[3] Probably early in January, 1804, or possibly the end of December, 1803.

[4] The title page for the first edition of Op. 42 is reproduced here from a microfilm copy of the original, which is in the Peters Bibliothek at Leipzig (No. 10867). Note the reference to the trio as *Notturno*, corrected in the later editions. A relatively late re-engraved edition (1858), ". . . nouvelle et soigneusement revue", was published under the imprint of C. F. Peters (successor to Hoffmeister & Kühnel). The work appeared in score, whereas in the first edition only the two separate parts were printed.

[5] *Thematisches Verzeichniss der Compositionen für Instrumental musik . . . I. Heft Louis van Beethoven . . . Leipzig, bei Friedr[ich] Hofmeister,* 1819.

[6] The first edition of this revised catalogue, according to Riemann, appeared in 1864. However, no copy can be located. It is extremely doubtful that the information is correct.

[7] "nicht von [Beethoven] gemacht, sondern nur von ihm durchgesehen und 'stellenweise' verbessert worden."

[8] Unfortunately, the letter from Hoffmeister, to which this is a reply, is lost.

[9] Curiously enough, when this letter was first published in the *Neue Zeitschrift für Musik* (1837, Vol. 6, p. 83), by C. G. S. Böhme, head of C. F. Peters, it was remarked that the word "Uebersetzungen" (here translated "transcriptions") referred to translations for a collection (4 volumes) of Italian and German songs or the "Italian and German Ariettas", Op. 82. This is evidently erroneous since the manuscript of one of the Ariettas is dated 6 years after the letter and the former collection has never been identified. Riemann (German edition of the Thayer biography) points out that Beethoven not infrequently used the word "Uebersetzungen" to mean arrangements or transcriptions.

[10] See footnote 15: On arrangements in general, Beethoven had this to say (*Wiener Zeitung*, October, 1800): "Arrangements are nowadays (in our prolific times) something an author only reluctantly submits to, but the least one can reasonably expect is that the publisher indicate it on the title page so as not to damage the reputation of the author or mislead the public."

[11] *Chronologisches Verzeichniss der Werke Ludwig van Beethovens.* Berlin, Ferdinand Schneider.

concerned.[12] In subsequent editions of the Thayer biography,[13] the editors quote the passage from the Hoffmeister letter in connection with Op. 41 and 42, giving it as conclusive proof that Beethoven authorized the publication and disavowed all but a small part in the making of the transcriptions.

Wilhelm Altmann[14] has conjectured that the viola piece was probably the work of Ferdinand Ries,[15] a pupil of Beethoven, and elsewhere it is suggested that Franz Xaver Kleinheinz was responsible for Op. 41,[16] but whether or not these men or some Viennese hacks were the actual transcribers, it is reasonably certain that the arrangements were not done by the composer himself.

A study of the Notturno reveals a good deal to support this contention. On close analysis, it appears extremely doubtful that the composer spent much time on this arrangement or that the revision could have gone, at most, beyond the correction of a few details. Aside from numerous examples of bad taste, the awkward writing for the keyboard could hardly have met with his approval, had he cared to take the trouble to examine it critically. Neither could he have been pleased (especially since he played the instrument himself) with the colorless treatment of the viola, even in an arrangement ostensibly nothing more than a piano solo piece with an obbligato viola part. These very weaknesses may account for the apparent lack of interest in the arrangement and its disappearance from publishers' catalogues after 1890.[17]

The present edition represents a completely new adaptation for viola and piano of the Serenade, Op. 8. Convinced of the remarkable suitability of the music for the purpose, the Editor has gone back to Beethoven's original score and endeavored to transcribe it as faithfully as possible in terms of the two instruments, while at the same time attempting to create a balanced piece of chamber music. It is hoped that in its new form the Notturno may prove a useful addition to the violist's limited repertoire.

SYDNEY BECK

---

[12] Op. 42, was, for some reason, completely ignored in the first edition of Thayer's *Life*, 1872. See Footnote 15.

[13] A. W. Thayer—*Ludwig van Beethoven's Leben* (translated by Deiters and revised by Riemann, 1910, Vol. 2, p. 50); *The Life of Ludwig van Beethoven* (edited by H. E. Krehbiel, 1921, Vol. 1, p. 208).

[14] Cobbett, *Cyclopedic Survey of Chamber Music* (1930, Vol. 2, p. 517). Altmann later changed his mind and cited Beethoven as the probable arranger. He conceded, however, the impossibility of such an assumption in the case of Op. 41. (*Die Musik*, 1934, Vol. 26, p. 350.)

[15] In the *Biographische Notizen über Ludwig van Beethoven* by Wegeler and Ries (1838 ed., p. 93, 94; Kallischer's reprint, 1906, p. 122, 113), Ries says that Beethoven made the arrangements of only four of his works himself, and these do not include the Serenade or Notturno. (Thayer's early uncertainty may be attributed to the remarks of Ries to whom he refers in his *Verzeichniss* of 1865.) He adds: "Many other things were arranged by me, looked over by Beethoven and then sold by his brother, Caspar, under Beethoven's name." Ries is not always reliable. However, since we know that Caspar had nothing to do with the selling of Op. 41 and 42 to Hoffmeister, it does not necessarily follow that Ries did not make the arrangements.

[16] D. W. MacArdle, *A Checklist of Beethoven's Chamber Music*. (*Music & Letters*, Jan., 1946.)

[17] Several editions of the Notturno were published during the 19th century, all more or less adhering to the original arrangement. A copy of the 1858 Peters edition of the work is in the New York Public Library. The Editor owns a copy published by F. P. Dunst, Frankfurt, probably around 1830, in which there is no indication that the work is an arrangement.

Title page of the First Edition of the Notturno for Pianoforte and Viola, Op. 42

NOTTURNO
for Viola and Piano

Ludwig van Beethoven, Op.42
Revised and edited by Sydney Beck

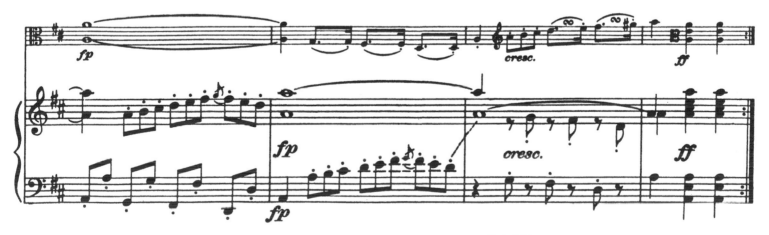

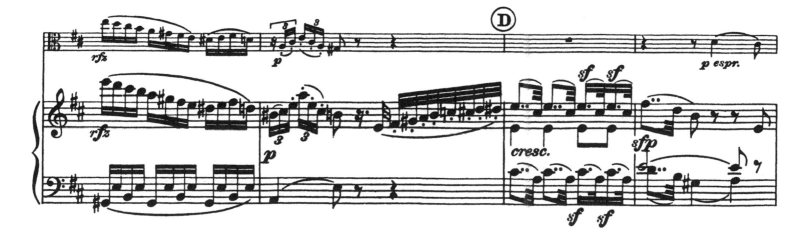

Minuetto
Allegretto

Trio

*Menuétto da capo
e poi la Coda*

Coda

Adagio

attacca

Scherzo
Allegro molto

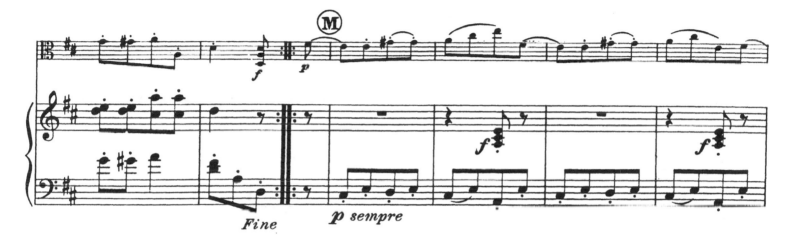

Adagio. Tempo primo

attacca

Scherzo
Allegro molto

Adagio. Tempo primo

Allegretto alla Polacca

NOTTURNO
for Viola and Piano

Viola

Ludwig van Beethoven, Op.42
Revised and edited by Sydney Beck

Viola

Viola

Marcia
Allegro

18

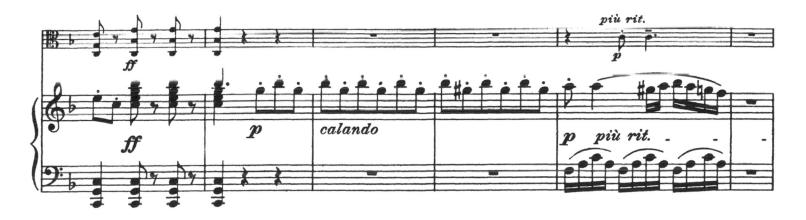

Andante quasi Allegretto

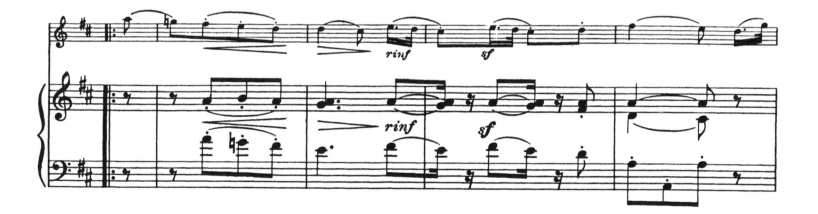

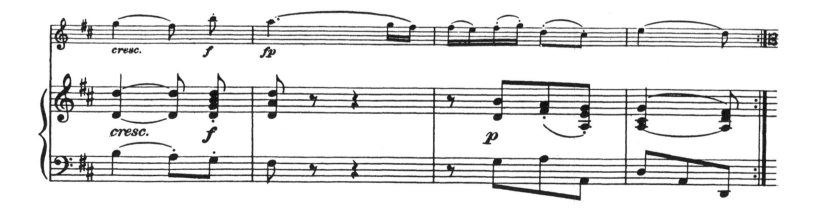

Var. 1

Var. 2

Var. 3

Var. 4

Allegro

Tempo I°

Marcia
Allegro